perfect harmony

A MUSICAL JOURNEY WITH

THE BOYS CHOIR OF HARLEM

perfect harmony

A MUSICAL JOURNEY WITH

THE BOYS CHOIR OF HARLEM

POEMS AND PHOTOGRAPHS BY

charles r. smith, jr.

JUMP AT THE SUN

HYPERION BOOKS FOR CHILDREN

NEW YORK

Printed in Hong Kong

First Edition
3 5 7 9 10 8 6 4 2

LIBRARY OF CONGRESS CATALOGING-IN-PUBLICATION DATA
Smith, Charles R., Jr.
Perfect harmony: a musical journey with the Boys Choir of Harlem: poems and
photographs by Charles R. Smith, Jr.— 1st ed.
p.   cm.
Summary: A collection of poems that capture the feelings and expression of music in
some of its forms.
ISBN 0-7868-0758-X
1. Music—Juvenile poetry. 2. Children's poetry, American. 3. Boys Choir of Harlem—
Pictorial works—Juvenile literature. [1. Music—Poetry. 2. American poetry.] I. Title.
PS3619.M57 H3 2002
811'.6—dc21
2001042277

Visit www.jumpatthesun.com

CONTENTS

This is dedicated to anyone and everyone who loves music in all its many shapes and forms, and to all the musicians who create it

Focus

Feet apart

arms at sides

chest puffed out

head held high

w a i t i n g

to release butterflies
inside.

Eyes focus

like

the calm

before the storm

ready to erupt

before I perform

toes tingle

feet quake

muscles twitch

hands shake

while

throat hums

hummmmmmms

hummmmmmmmmmmmmmmms

so that

my voice may

awake.

Focus

I must

focus

to channel my

electricity

and relax

r e l a x
r e l a x

before I set

the butterflies

free.

DEEP BREATHS

Ex-
hale
s l o w.
In-
hale
d e e p.
Thoughts focus.
Ready.
Release.

Breath
breathes life
into words
on a page
gives them
a stage
to showcase
sound

and express
rage
drown sorrows
and engage
ears
with musical
notes
that jump
leap
and
shout
from throats
voicing words
floating
on air
built up
in lungs
singing

singing
a song
that began
with a breath
transformed
from air
to notes
to words
in voice
waiting
to be
sung.

Energy spent.
Ex-
hale
and
done.

Tempo

If-the-tempo-is-too-fast-it-makes-your-words-crash-and-causes-your-song-to-sound-like-trash.

But . . .

If
the
tem-
po
is
too
slow
you
lose
the
flow,
you
know?

So . . .

Keep the tempo at a moderate pace.
Let the music be your guide and don't chase.

Not too fast or too slow,
just let the words go
with just the right pattern of tempo.

11

RHYTHM IS

Drumsticks tick
tick tick tick
rhythmic licks
with a flick
of the wrist.
Like the thump
of a drum
rhythm hums
a track
for voices
to glide
slide and
ride
upon.
Creating constant sound
with a background
beat,
rhythm is the
clock
that keeps
vocal cords
on their feet.
Setting lyrics
in motion,
rhythm is
an ocean
filled with
the

pump-pump
pump-pump
sound of
heartbeats
the
jump-jump
jump-jump
of double-Dutch
feet
keeping time
with rope
skip
skip
skipping on concrete
the
dribble-dribble
stop
that makes jumpshots
drop
the
pop-pop
pop-pop-pop
sound of kernels
getting hot.
From a nod

of the head
to a
  shake
shake
  shake
of
the feet
rhythm lives in you
rhythm lives in me
rhythm in the song of life
breaks
breaks
down
to one
simple key:
marching your own
voice
to your own
rhythmic
beat.

Soprano Haiku

Songbirds sing in sweet
soprano voices; hitting
high notes easily.

ALTO HAIKU

Alto notes drift high

in the sky lingering

beneath soprano wings.

FLYiNG SOLo

All eyes on me
I part the
sea
of harmony
setting butterflies
free
crooning
honey-drenched notes
in my
sweet
alto key.
Center stage
I engage
ears
with emotion
not found
on a page.

Heartstrings
I pluck
and tug
with conviction,
using attitude,
feeling,
presence, and
diction.
Stepping to the
front
with confidence,
talent,
and soul

flying solo
has always been
my goal.

Tenor Haiku

Not too heavy, not
too soft, tenor hits notes like
a velvet hammer.

BaSS HaiKu

Buried in the deep
reaches of the belly; bass
booms deep and heavy.

HARMONY

A perfect marriage of rhythm and time,
voices blend to create harmonic rhyme.

Bass drops anchor in musical sea,
for tenor and alto to create harmony.

Soprano chimes in with high notes that soar,
bass booms deep to even the score.

Tenor pitches words so nat-u-rally,
while alto floats in smooth and gracefully.

Soprano she flies so high in the sky,
as alto hovers below and nearby.

Each voice shines bright like glass in the sun,
harmony brings them together as one.

When musical notes melt with precision and pace,
music has life, energy, and grace.

B-FLAT BOOGiE

B-FLAT BOOGIE and
bebop beats course through veins
like electricity.

B-FLAT BOOGIE and
bebop beats bounce beautiful
bodies in plush seats.

B-FLAT BOOGIE and
bebop beats vibrate notes from
instrument to ear
to brain to heartbeat to soul
soothed by satin-soft sound.

B-FLAT BOOGIE and
bebop beats set a trail of
emotions on fire.

B-FLAT BOOGIE and
bebop beats swing on ballroom
floors with elegance.

B-FLAT BOOGIE and
bebop beats paint vibrant brush-
strokes of emotion
over canvas of faces
with palette of heartfelt blues.

B-FLAT BOOGIE and
bebop beats flit like humming
birds dancing in trees.

B-FLAT BOOGIE and
bebop beats breathe life into
exhausted spirits.

B-FLAT BOOGIE and
bebop beats simmer slowly
over hungry ears
like hot bubbling gumbo
setting senses on fire.

Sing Me a Song

Rhythm and rhyme

aren't worth a dime

if your voice don't swing

and make hearts climb.

    Belt out a tune

    bounce to the beat,

    make me clap loud

    and jump out my seat.

Tempo and time

aren't worth a dime,

if your notes are flat

and your words don't shine.

    Spin 'em around

    toss 'em up high

    let your notes soar

    make the song fly.

It makes no difference

if you're big or small,

just inhale deeply

and

give it your alllllll.

It don't

really matter

if your high notes

can make glass shatter

just . . .

    Belt out a tune

    bounce to the beat,

    make me clap loud

    and jump out my seat.

Yeah!

ONE MIGHTY VOICE

It all begins
with the power
of one
when notes
are hit
and
words are sung
when lyrics
slide off
the tip of the
tongue
their strength
grows strong
from the power
of one.
One voice brings joy.
One voice brings pain.
One voice brings laughter.
One voice brings rain-
soaked lyrics
that make
dry eyes
drip
working

together
to make
hearts
skip.
Energy
and attitude
glow
from throats
one voice
at a time,
like rays
from the
sun
together
they shine.
One plus
one
plus one
plus
more
equals
one large
collective
mighty ROAR!

MUSICAL TERMS

Alto—the low singing voice of a woman or young boy, between the soprano and tenor.

Bass—the lowest male singing voice, or the lowest instrument of any instrumental family.

Bebop—a style of jazz that originated in the 1940s featuring improvisation, complex rhythms, and fast tempos.

Blues—a form of African American folk music that came from spirituals and work songs.

Bright—a term used to describe a voice as high and clear.

Chime—to make a harmonious musical sound; to make a ringing sound when struck; a bell or set of bells.

Choir—an organized group of singers.

Croon—to hum or sing softly.

Diction—the choice and use of words in speech and writing.

Flat—a note that is lowered by a half step; sung or played too low and out of tune.

Harmony—a combination of sounds considered pleasing to the ear; a combination of tones sounded simultaneously.

Improvise —to make up on the spot without practice or preparation.

Key—the system of tones and harmonies based on a seven-note major or minor scale.

Lyrics—the words of a song.

Melody—a pleasing, usually rhythmic, sequence of single notes.

Note—the symbol used to notate a single musical sound.

Pitch—the highness or lowness of a musical sound.

Presence—the ability to command attention in a public space.

Rhythm—a regular pattern formed by a series of sounds with different lengths and accents.

Scale—an arrangement of tones in a specific order of whole steps and half steps.

Score—the written form of a piece of music for orchestral or vocal parts, either complete or for a single instrument or voice.

Soprano—the highest singing voice of a woman or a young boy.

Staccato—sung or played in an abrupt or disconnected fashion.

Swing—to play with energy and natural rhythm; a form of big-band jazz music popular in the 1930s and '40s.

Tempo—the speed at which music is or should be played.

Tenor—a high adult male singing voice, between the alto and bass.

POETIC TERMS

Antonym—a word having a meaning opposite to that of another word.

Cadence—the pace at which a poem moves; a figure of speech that gives a feeling of closure.

Couplet—a couple, or pair, of lines of poetry, usually rhymed. (See "Harmony.")

Haiku—a Japanese lyric poem usually having three unrhymed lines of five, seven, and five syllables; a haiku may be numbered or untitled.

Homonym—one or two or more words that have the same sound but different meanings (for example: to, too, two).

Imagery—vivid language used to create a picture. (See "Rhythm Is.")

Metaphor—a figure of speech in which one thing is used to represent another. (See "Rhythm Is.")

Meter—the rhythmic pattern of a poem determined by the kind and number of lines.

Simile—a comparison of one thing with another using *like* or *as*. (See "Tenor Haiku.")

Slang—informal words used in place of standard words for effect.

Stanza—a group of lines of verse.

Synonym—a word with nearly the same meaning as another.

Verse—a line of poetry.

Tanka—a Japanese lyric poem similar to a haiku, but longer. (See "B-flat Boogie," stanzas 3, 6, and 9.)

Acknowledgments & Thank-Yous

The book you now hold in your hands is the result of a great deal of time, energy, and effort spent that involved the assistance of several people.

Before I thank anyone, I have to start with my editor, Andrea Davis Pinkney, who helped turn an idea into a reality. Thanks for keeping the poems on track as well.

It all began with Nadine Heron-Fortune and Horace Turnbull, who helped put me in contact with all of the people I needed to speak to. Mr. Turnbull was as gracious as ever in letting me do my thing and taught me more than a few things about music in general and life in particular. To Laurie Potter, for teaching me the basics of music theory. To William Bird, Terry Wright, Walter Rutledge, and Mr. Butler, for all the great memories we share from Skidmore. To David Crone, for allowing me access to finish what I started. To Larry Robinson and Frank Jones, for all their help. To Keith the "Piano Man," for all his enthusiasm and for allowing me to pick his brain. To Randall Bess Gregoire, for all his input on what makes a great soloist; "Flying Solo" uses many of the feelings you so perfectly described.

And last but certainly not least, to Dr. Walter Turnbull and to all of the boys of the Boys Choir of Harlem, who allowed me into their world and welcomed me as one of their own without restraint. It was a pleasure to meet and photograph you and help spread the message of music. Good luck to you in all of your endeavors. With such a solid foundation, I know you will go far.